INSIDE THE EARTH

Also available in Piccolo Colour Books

A PICCOLO COLOUR BOOK

INSIDE
THE EARTH

by ROSE WYLER and GERALD AMES

from Planet Earth

PAN BOOKS LTD : LONDON

EDITORIAL ADVISERS

JOSETTE FRANK, Director for Children's Books,
Child Study Association of America
DR LELAND B. JACOBS, Professor of Education,
Teachers College, Columbia University

First published in Great Britain by
Paul Hamlyn as *Inside the Earth*.

This edition first published 1971 by
Pan Books Ltd, 33 Tothill Street, London, S.W.1.

ISBN 0 330 02803 0

© Copyright 1968, 1960 by
Western Publishing Company Inc

CREDITS

Diagrams by Cornelius DeWitt;
Mineral Drawings by Raymond Perlman
The Anaconda Company, 59
Horace Bristol-FPG, 67
Environmental Science Services Administration, 35
David-Forbet—Shostal, 66
General Dynamics, 79
General Electric Research & Development Centre, 13
Wilson & MacPherson Hole, 45
Icelandic Airlines, 71
Lt Alan Lisle, 26
Joseph Muench, 28
National Park Service, 24
South Dakota Department of Highways, 11
Standard Oil Company (New Jersey), 8, 46, 48, 61
Harold Wanless, 37
Westinghouse Electric Corporation, 74
Wide World Photos, 32
Rose Wyler and Gerald Ames, 14, 19, 20

Printed in Italy

CONTENTS

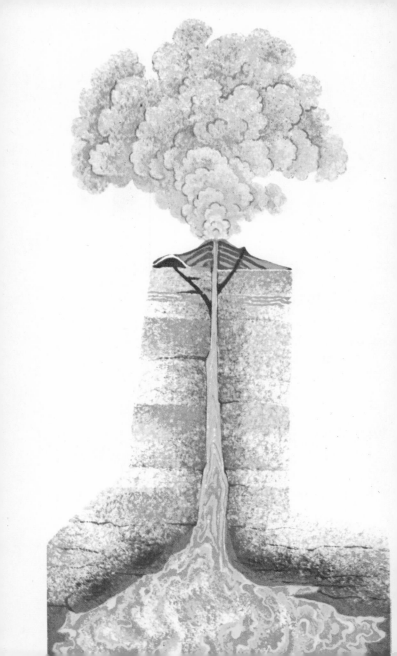

THE DARK REALM

THE air has its storms; the ocean has its waves and tides. By comparison, the solid earth seems quiet, but this quiet is often broken by earthquakes and volcanic eruptions. Lava pours from the depths. Mountains explode. The planet quivers like a steel spring. The ground shakes, and cities fall in ruins.

These disturbances begin deep inside the earth. What forces set them off? Men cannot get into the interior to find out. That dark realm is for ever closed by the pressure of the rock load above it. Only a few miles down, pressure would squeeze together the walls of any shaft or tunnel.

Yet the interior has been explored in other ways. As a doctor listens with his stethoscope to what is going on inside a patient, scientists 'listen' with instruments to what is going on inside the planet.

Here in this book you will read about their investigations. You will follow scientists in the field and in the laboratory as they study the mighty forces that shape our earth.

Temperature in drill holes increases with depth

Clues From Volcanoes

1. LIVELY ROCK

WHEN prospectors drill for oil, they often have trouble with underground heat. The deeper they drill, the hotter the rock. Everywhere in the world the temperature increases with depth. It rises faster in some places than others, but the average increase is one degree Centigrade for every 100 feet. Two miles down in the gold mines of South Africa, the rock walls are so hot that only a powerful air-conditioning system keeps the miners from being roasted alive.

Temperatures have been taken only as far down as the deepest bore holes–about five miles. From there on, the rock probably continues to get hotter at the same rate. If so, the temperature 25 miles down would be 1,200 degrees. This is hotter than a blast furnace. In fact, it is hotter than the melting points of rocks at the earth's surface.

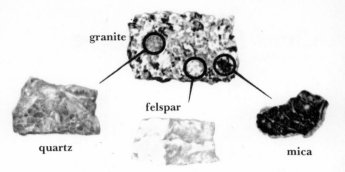

granite

quartz

felspar

mica

Can it be that the earth beneath the surface is liquid? Liquid lava pours from volcanoes, but this does not prove that the whole interior is liquid. Hot as it is, it shows signs of being solid, or mostly solid.

WHEN ROCK FREEZES

To scientists, ice is a kind of rock. Do you know how ice forms? Before water cools to its freezing point, the water molecules are loose and jostling one another. But at the freezing point they quieten down and join together, forming crystals.

Most of the earth's rock is made of crystals. There are many kinds of crystal, each made of a different mineral substance.

To learn how crystals form in rock, scientists melt a mixture of minerals and watch as it cools. The substance with the highest freezing point is the first to start forming crystals.

Then other substances reach their freezing points and begin to crystallize.

Melted rock that pours from the earth as lava usually freezes in a few hours. As a result of this quick freezing, the crystals are tiny. They have no time to grow large.

The story is different when melted rock stays underground and cools off slowly. During the long cooling, more and more atoms join on to the crystals, which keep on growing. Examine a piece of granite and notice its large, clearly outlined crystals. They show that the rock formed deep in the earth, from a rock melt that cooled slowly.

Granite rocks surrounding a lake

As a rock melt crystallizes, it shrinks. That is because its atoms pack close together in the crystals. But melting rock expands because its jostling atoms spread farther apart.

In order to melt, rock *must* expand. It must push harder than the pressure surrounding it. At the surface, this is easy, since the only pressure is that of the atmosphere–about 15 pounds per square inch. But 30 miles inside the earth, the weight of overlying rock creates a pressure greater than 200,000 pounds per square inch.

Scientists have shown how rock behaves under high pressure. They squeeze a sample in a powerful press, then heat it. Even when heated beyond its ordinary melting point, the rock stays solid. It does not have enough energy to overcome the pressure around it. Only when the rock gets much hotter–when its atoms become very lively and agitated–does it expand and melt.

Inside the earth, rock often heats up to a point where it has the energy to melt and gush from volcanoes. In fact, it sometimes explodes, shattering mountains.

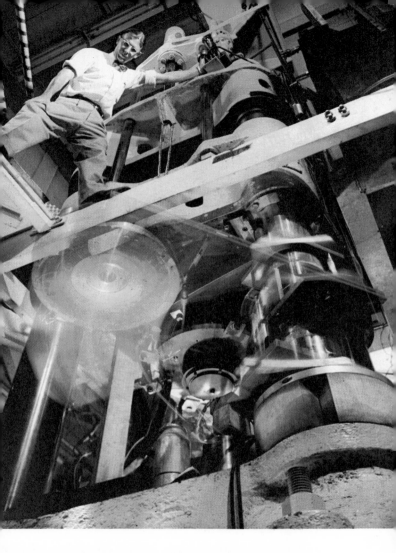

**Rocks and minerals are tested in a press at temperatures
of thousands of pounds per square inch**

The volcano Pelée is quiet now, but in 1902 it destroyed the city of St Pierre, Martinique

2. MOUNTAIN THAT EXPLODED

In the year 1902 an old, quiet volcano on the island of Martinique, in the West Indies, came to life in a terrible way. The people of Martinique can never forget how it destroyed their city, St Pierre, and in one dreadful minute killed the 28,000 inhabitants.

St Pierre was a busy seaport. Offshore, ships could always be seen loading sugar and rum. The cane from which these products were made grew on plantations spreading over the slopes and valleys behind the city.

Five miles to the north rose a mountain named Pelée. The islanders knew it was an old volcano. It had fumed a little fifty years earlier, but since then had been quiet and harmless.

Pelée was not shaped like a regular cone. Before historic times its top had caved in, leaving a hollow about half a mile across. Water had once filled the hollow, but it was dry now, so people called it the Dry Pond.

THE AWAKENING

One day towards the end of April, 1902, a plume of vapour rose from Pelée, and some light dust fell on villages nearby. Once in a while the ground trembled as a low rumbling came from the mountain. This caused no alarm. The same things had happened

Pelée's cone collapsed long ago

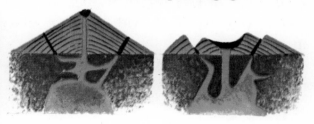

fifty years earlier and nothing worse had followed. Students and teachers at the local school discussed the mountain's behaviour. They compared Pelée to Vesuvius, the volcano that destroyed the ancient city of Pompeii.

The volcano gradually came to life

Boys and girls joined parties of sightseers and climbed to the top of Pelée. The Dry Pond had filled with water. Trees growing there were nearly submerged, with only their tops showing. In the middle of the pond rose a cone made of lava fragments. Jets of water spurted from it, along with puffs of dusty vapour.

Gradually, the mountain became more violent. One night there were several explosions.

The wall of the Dry Pond collapsed, leaving a V-shaped gap. Water rushed through the gap, forming a deluge of mud that poured down the valley and swept houses and people into the sea.

Repeated flows of mud buried villages near the mountain. People fled to St Pierre for safety. Everywhere, a light grey dust fell like snow, covering the ground and weighing down the branches of trees. At night, clouds gleaming with an orange light rolled from the summit. Glowing blocks of lava burst out of the mountain and hurtled down its slopes.

Then came the eighth of May and the eruption that brought death to St Pierre.

DAY OF DESTRUCTION

Afterwards, a man who lived a mile from the city told what he saw that morning. At first there was only the usual vapour rising over the mountain. Then something spurted from the summit–a jet of ash and hot gas.

The jet raced downhill. Behind it rose a wall of cloud. In a minute and a half the cloud rolled to St Pierre and covered the city.

Meanwhile, the watcher felt a blast of wind from the cloud.

This wind saved the lives of some sailors aboard ships at anchor. It threw them into the sea before the cloud reached them. When the cloud came, it scalded them about the head and shoulders, but the parts of their bodies underwater were unharmed.

In St Pierre the sudden blast of wind tumbled houses and buried their occupants in the ruins. Stoves and lamps set the wreckage ablaze. The whole city became a furnace.

A RESCUE

During the following week, rescue parties searched the ruins. Under the dust and rubble they found a sheet of paper with a student's notes about Vesuvius and the destruction of Pompeii.

One man, a shoemaker, was found alive. It seemed that not another soul had survived. But on the fourth day the searchers heard cries coming from the dungeon of the city prison. When they broke through the door a young prisoner was there, waiting.

**People of St Pierre died where
these ruins stand**

Louis Cyparis had been sentenced to a month in jail for getting into a fight. Near the end of the month he was let out to do a day's work, but instead of coming back

**Steamy vapours escape from the side of
La Soufrière volcano, Guadeloupe**

in the evening he stayed out all night. When
he returned the next morning the warden shut
him up in the dungeon. To this punishment,
Louis Cyparis owed his life.

Telling his story afterwards, Louis said that on the morning of the disaster he suddenly heard people scream and cry out that they were burning. Then there was silence.

'A vapour rushed in through the little window over my door,' Louis said. 'It burned so much that I jumped around everywhere trying to get away from it.'

Louis had burns on his back and other parts of his body, but his clothing was unharmed. The vapour had no odour, he said. The sailors agreed about this. They compared their burns to scalds from steam, and thought the vapour of the cloud must have been steam or something like it.

WHY SO EXPLOSIVE

After May 8th there were many similar eruptions of Pelée, which were observed by the French scientist, Alexandre Lacroix. Each time, ash and gas spurted through the heap of material at the summit. As the fluid raced downwards, vapour billowing from it formed a dark wall of cloud.

Clearly, the fluid was highly charged with gases. Inside the volcano, the gases were held in the lava under pressure, as gas is held in soda-water when the bottle is capped. But once the stuff was outside, the gases bubbled out violently. Boiling against the ground, they formed a vapour cushion on which the mixture floated downhill.

Pumice is a bubbly froth turned solid

Gobs of lava were carried up in the cloud. Foaming and freezing at once, they turned into a glassy froth, called pumice. Millions of frozen bubbles burst in the air, and their fragments drifted down as dust.

Pelée's explosiveness was due largely to the stiffness of the lava. Most of it emerged as nearly solid chunks that clogged the volcano's mouth. Deeper down, more lava was accumulating. When the pressure of its bottled-up gases reached a certain point, the mixture blasted out through a weak part of the summit.

3. FLOODS OF LAVA

ANOTHER type of volcano erupts a more fluid, less explosive lava, which flows quite far before turning solid. Because the outpourings spread widely, they form a broad mountain with gentle slopes.

Such a volcano, Mauna Loa, caps the island of Hawaii. The whole island, in fact, is built of the volcano's lava. The vast dark pile, resting on the ocean floor, rises 16,000 feet to the surface–over three miles–then another 13,700 feet above the surface.

The summit of Mauna Loa usually remains quiet while lava drains from cracks in its sides. But twenty miles from the summit is a very active companion, Kilauea.

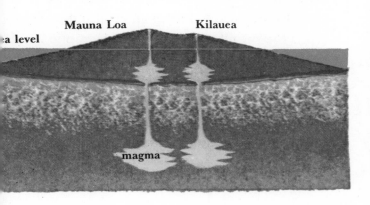

**Lava bubbles up through the
crater floor at Kilauea**

Here scientists have an observatory for studying the volcano's behaviour.

The top of Kilauea caved in long ago,
leaving a steep-walled pit two miles across.
Lava rises into the pit through vents, or volcanic openings, in its floor. For many years
lava filled the pit, forming a molten lake. The
lake drained away during an eruption in 1924.
Later the pit filled up again, then emptied and
refilled time after time.

Fountains of lava often gushed up from
the lake, driven by frothing gases. What
gases? Scientists collected vapours fuming
around the lake and found they were mainly
steam.

WATER IN ROCK

Where does the steam come from? There is water that lies in cracks within the earth's crust and there is water that actually exists within rock. When granite, for example, is melted in the laboratory, water vapour is driven from it. Water often accounts for more than two per cent of the weight of granite. Some is enclosed in microscopic cavities between crystals, and some is linked right in the atom chains of the crystals themselves.

A great store of water lies imprisoned in the earth's rock. Wherever rock melts, the water turns into vapour, which remains in the rock melt.

WORK OF LAVA

Scientists at Kilauea watch for signs of activity beneath the mountain, in order to warn people of expected eruptions. When lava starts to drive upwards, it jolts the surrounding rock. Vibrations go from there to the surface, where they are recorded by instruments. The records show that disturbances start around 35 miles beneath the surface.

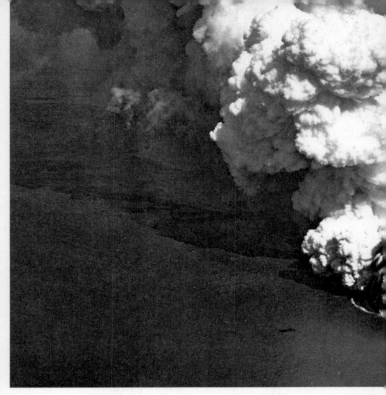

This, the scientists conclude, is the depth from which lava begins its journey.

In the course of millions of years, eruptions from under the ocean at Hawaii have piled up 100,000 cubic miles of rock. The Hawaiian lava forms a dark, fine-grained rock called basalt. A high content of iron makes it heavy and somewhat magnetic.

Similar outpourings have built a chain of

Basalt

**A volcano emerges
from the sea,
forming a new island
in the Azores**

islands to the north-west. They are the high
points of an underwater ridge, formed from
lava which has erupted through cracks in the
ocean floor.

In other parts of the world also, undersea
volcanoes are at work. Occasionally, one of
them breaks above the surface, shoving up a
dark mass of lava amid billowing steam. Thus,
a new island is born.

27

Lava has flooded parts of continents, as well as the ocean floor. The Antrim Plateau of Northern Ireland is covered by over 1,000 square miles of basalt lava. This is only part, however, of a vast area of lavas, now much of it beneath the sea, which extends to Greenland, Iceland, and the Faröes. The lavas were erupted from long fissures.

Flowing lava cooled to form strange landscape at Craters of the Moon, Idaho, USA

Uranium and a few other elements are naturally radioactive. Their atoms break down, one after another, and in doing so release heat. Such elements are found in granite, basalt, and other rocks that once lay deep in the earth.

In a body of rock that has lain undisturbed for millions of years, the radioactive elements are always breaking down and releasing heat. Eventually, the rock may get so hot that it begins to melt.

In places above the hot rock, there are cracks or other weaknesses. The hot rock pushes into these places, slowly expanding and becoming half liquid. In this state it is called *magma*, after the Greek word for dough. The magma slowly oozes upwards.

Water vapour and other gases are dissolved in the magma. They start to bubble out, making the magma into a frothy lava that blasts to the surface. As this material erupts, some of the pressure below is removed, allowing more of the deep magma to liquefy and rise. Soon a flood of molten rock is pouring from the earth.

What Earthquakes Tell

4. TREMBLING EARTH

WITHOUT any warning, a great thumping blow strikes our planet. This is the first shock of an earthquake. The ground heaves like a monster in convulsions. People are thrown flat on their faces. Houses topple, bridges fall, mountain crags collapse.

The earth has several zones where earthquakes occur often. One of them runs the

length of South America, along the Andes Mountains and the shore of the Pacific. Every country in this zone has suffered from earthquakes–Chile most of all.

In 1939, Chile was jolted by a powerful earthquake that shattered towns and killed 30,000 people. Houses and bridges were rebuilt, and everyone hoped they would be strong enough to withstand future earthquakes. But disaster came again in 1960. Before dawn on May 21st, the people of the city of Concepción, awakened by the shaking of their houses, had to run out of doors to escape falling roofs and walls.

The Chilean earthquake of 1960 caused this destruction

The first shock was felt throughout southern Chile. During the rest of the day and the following night the ground frequently trembled with after-shocks. Then, on May 22nd, came the most powerful shock of all. It originated about 200 miles south of Concepción, from some disturbance under the sea. This shock dumped cliffs into valleys, toppled buildings, and killed thousands of people.

The disturbance under the sea caused one of the most dreaded effects of earthquakes. This was a great sea wave, for which scientists use the Japanese word *tsunami*.

A tsunami wave starts from the bottom, where it is launched by a heaving of the sea floor. It reaches the surface and spreads out in a widening circle, followed by other waves. These waves are only one or two feet high, and pass under a ship without being noticed. But their length, from one wave crest to another, is 200 miles or more. Rushing at speeds of several hundred miles an hour, they cross the Pacific in a day.

The amount of water in a tsunami is enormous, and this makes it dangerous as it approaches land.

A shallow bottom slows the wave, causing it to build higher and higher. A harbour funnels it into a narrow space, forcing it to rise still higher. Finally, a rushing wall of water crashes over the shore, destroying whatever it hits.

Shocks of the Chilean earthquake were detected across the Pacific, in Hawaii and Japan.

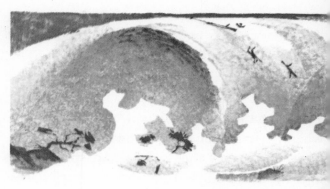

Sirens sounded a warning, but it was night and families were asleep. Many did not hear the alarm. When the tsunami struck, people in several harbours were killed.

Waterfronts of southern Chile bore the full brunt of the tsunami. Entire fishing fleets were lost with their crews. One harbour was hit by a 30-foot wave. People ran to high ground for safety, but a landslide swept them into the sea.

By the end of the cycle of earthquakes, several thousand Chileans had lost their lives, 50,000 homes and other buildings lay in ruins, and half a million more were damaged. All this destruction was brought about by events that happened 30 miles beneath the mountains and the sea.

A tsunami wave strikes the shore

A waterfront in Chile has been wrecked by the tsunami

Traces of surface movement can often be seen in a cliff or a road cutting.

If you find a crack that runs down across layers of rock, notice whether the layers are out of line. If they are–if the layers on one side of the crack are above or below the same layers on the opposite side–you can see that the rock has broken and moved. And when this movement happened, it caused an earthquake.

After an earthquake in Bombay, India, in 1819, the people were startled by a remarkable change. At a place where the land had cracked, the surface had risen 20 feet on one side of the crack and dropped 10 feet on the other side. Together, the vertical movements of the earth had produced a cliff 30 feet high.

During earthquakes that shake the coast of California every twenty years or so, movement is mainly horizontal. It occurs along a rift–a zone of cracks and dislocations–that runs north and south for several hundred miles.

**Displaced layers show how the
rock broke and moved**

After the great Californian earthquake of 1906, surveyors found that land on the west side of the rift had moved northwards, and land on the other side had moved southwards. Roads and fences that crossed an active crack were broken and carried out of line as much as 15 or 20 feet. In all, movement had taken place along a stretch 275 miles long and 10 miles wide.

SPRINGY ROCK

When a strip of spring steel is bent, the energy that bends it is stored in the spring. If the steel is bent so far that it breaks, the energy is released and the broken sections jump back.

Inside the earth, rock behaves in the same way. It is bent by forces pressing or pulling on it, and this goes on for a long time, perhaps for hundreds of years. At the earth's surface nothing seems to be happening. But deep down, the rock is being gradually deformed–bent out of shape. If it becomes strained to the limit of its strength, it suddenly breaks. The broken sections snap back, and this rebound sets off an earthquake.

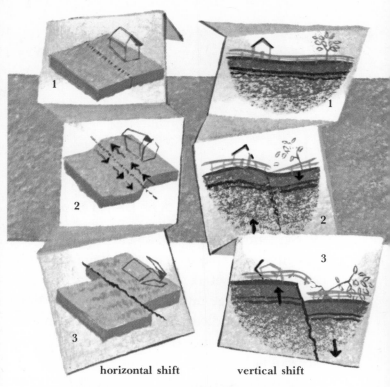

horizontal shift   vertical shift

**When rock under strain breaks, the broken
sections rebound, causing an earthquake**

The first shock may trigger breaks in other
places where the rock is strained. Shock follows upon shock, tormenting the disaster zone
for hours, days, weeks. At last, when the
greatest strains have been relieved, the earth
becomes quiet again.

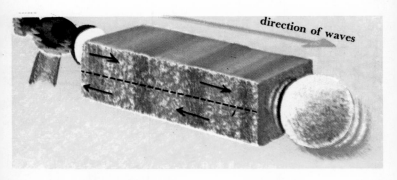

direction of waves

5. PORTRAIT OF AN EARTHQUAKE

ON September 1st, 1923, an earthquake struck the city of Tokyo. Houses collapsed and cooking fires set the wreckage ablaze. Families took refuge in a public square. While they were huddled there, a wind swept the fire over them and their possessions, killing thousands.

The very instruments for recording earthquakes were knocked out of operation. Scientists stayed at their stations and set them running again. Not knowing whether their own families were alive or dead, they worked to save the records so valuable to the nation and the world. Such records may lead to ways of predicting earthquakes, so that people can be warned in time and reach places of safety.

FREE

**Collect 6 coupons
and you'll get
a PAN Piccolo
absolutely free!**

What an offer!
Just choose any title
from the fascinating new
Piccolo Series, some of which
are listed on the next page.
Then fill in the coupon,
send it off with five others
—and you'll get your
PAN Piccolo absolutely free!

Piccolo free offer

To: Pan Books Ltd., 33 Tothill St., London, S.W.1.

Please send me my free copy of.........................
(you need only fill in the title once and attach 5 other
coupons)

NAME...

ADDRESS..

....

....

....

This offer, which is available only in the U.K. and the Republic of
Ireland, closes on December 31st, 1971.

Piccolo

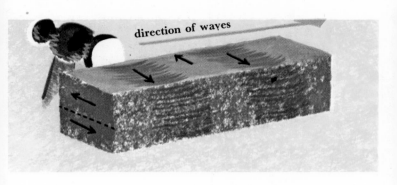

direction of waves

LEFT: compression waves are sent through steel
RIGHT: waves are sent sideways through steel

VIBRATION WAVES

The science of earthquakes is called seismology, from the Greek word *seismos*, earthquake. The main instrument used for studying earthquakes, the seismograph, records vibrations sent through the earth by shocks.

You can observe similar vibrations in a steel rod. Lay the rod down and place a ping-pong ball against one end. Hit the other end with a hammer. Notice how the ball bobbles and rattles against the rod. What is happening in the rod?

When you strike it, the steel at the end of the rod is compressed. Then, being springy, or elastic, it quickly jumps back.

By this movement the steel in the neighbouring section is compressed, and it, too, rebounds. Thus, the compression and rebound are passed through the rod. Meanwhile, the first section again compresses and jumps back. It does this over and over again. So does every other section.

As a result, a whole series of compressions travel through the rod. These are compression waves.

Another type of wave can be set off by striking the rod on the side. A section of the steel is knocked sideways, then jumps back. This shakes the neighbouring section, which shakes the next, and so a wave of shaking motion travels through the rod from end to end.

RECORDING EARTHQUAKE WAVES

An earthquake sends both types of waves zinging through the earth. At great distances the small, rapid vibrations cannot be felt, but the seismograph detects them.

In principle, the instrument is a pendulum. One kind of seismograph has the pendulum hanging like a gate from a gatepost. The

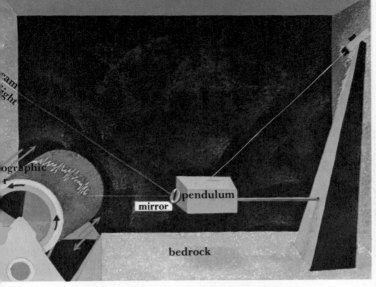

A seismograph detects earthquake waves

post is tilted a little towards the pendulum so the weight will hang at rest in one position. The post is mounted on bedrock in an underground vault.

Facing the pendulum is a rotating drum covered with photographic paper. The vault is dark, except for a narrow beam of light aimed at a mirror on the pendulum. The mirror reflects the beam to the drum. As the drum turns, the beam makes a line on the photographic paper. Even when the bedrock vibrates, the pendulum hangs practically motionless, so the light beam reflected by its mirror is steady. But the drum vibrates with the rock, and this makes the line on the photographic paper zig-zag. The wiggly line is a seismogram–the portrait of an earthquake.

SPEED AND DISTANCE

The waves from a distant earthquake arrive in groups. First come compression waves, the kind you set off by striking the end of a steel rod. Seismologists call them P-waves. 'P' stands for primary, meaning first to arrive. But it might as well mean 'push', since the vibration is a pushing motion. These waves are very fast. They travel at speeds of around 250 miles a minute.

Later come vibrations called S-waves. 'S' stands for secondary, meaning second to arrive. But it might as well mean 'shake', since these waves have a shaking motion, like the ones set off by striking the side of a steel rod.

The farther away the earthquake, the longer the time lag between the arrival of the P-waves and S-waves. Seismologists have prepared a table showing how long the second group lags behind the first at various distances. Here is a sample of figures from the table:

DISTANCE FROM EARTH- QUAKE CENTRE TO STATION miles	TIME LAG BETWEEN P-WAVES AND S-WAVES minutes	seconds
1,000	2	45
2,000	4	52
3,000	6	30
4,000	8	00
5,000	9	25
6,000	10	44

Suppose a seismogram shows a group of P-waves, then a group of S-waves that arrived 6 minutes and 30 seconds later. The seismologist knows what this means: an earthquake has occurred 3,000 miles away.

A scientist examines a seismogram

**Prospectors fire a seismic shot
to locate oil-bearing rock**

6. MESSAGES FROM THE DEPTHS

OIL prospectors have a method called 'seismic shooting' in which they use small artificial earthquakes. In the area they have chosen to explore, the prospectors bury a charge of dynamite. They plant detectors called geophones at various distances, and run wires from them to a recording instrument in a truck.

The surface rocks of the area are *sedimentary*. This means they are made of ancient sediments–sand and mud which came from the crumbling of earlier rocks. Where sedimentary rocks exist, they lie in layers on top of crystalline rocks like granite.

When the prospectors fire their 'shot', compression waves speed through the rock layers, hit the boundaries between them, and echo back. The returning waves reach the geophones,

An oil trap can be detected by seismic shooting

oil-bearing rock

where they set off electric signals. These go to the instrument in the truck, and are recorded as a seismogram.

Later, the seismogram is carefully studied. What will its zig-zag lines reveal? The prospectors look for signs of a structure they call an oil trap. Somewhere in the area, they believe, the layers of rock make an upward fold. One of the layers is sandstone, which may be soaked with oil and water. It is sandwiched between other layers through which the oil and water do not leak. The

A seismogram is examined for signs of an oil trap

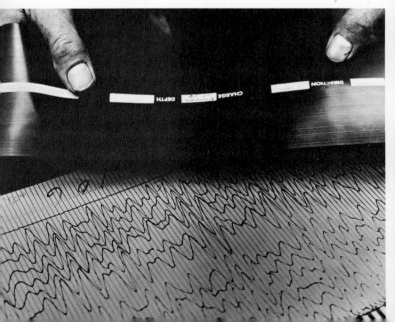

water in the sandstone forces the lighter oil to the top of the fold, and there it lies, trapped.

Such a structure can be located because waves from the shot hit the top of the fold and bounce back. Their arrival time is recorded. Since the speed of the waves is known, their travel time shows how far they have gone and where the fold is.

WHAT WAVE SPEEDS SHOW

Waves travel at different speeds in different rocks. When rock that is very elastic is compressed in a shock wave, it jumps back fast, so the wave goes fast. In a less elastic rock the reaction is slower, and so is the wave.

Scientists have learned from test shots just how fast compression waves travel in granite, sandstone, basalt, and other rocks. They can therefore tell from wave speeds the nature of rocks beyond their reach.

When seismic shots are made at sea, the waves travel under the ocean floor at a higher speed than waves passing through granite and other rocks of the continents.

They travel at the speed of waves in basalt. Is the rock under the oceans basalt? A few samples have been drilled from the ocean floor, and they have indeed turned out to be basalt.

In 1909 the Yugoslav seismologist, Andrija Mohorovicic, made an important discovery. Seismic waves speed up gradually as they go deeper, but at certain levels they make sudden changes in speed. They also change direction.

A level at which these changes happen is called a *discontinuity*. It seems to mark a boundary between different kinds of material. Several discontinuities have been found. The first important one lies about 20 miles down under the continents, and as little as three miles down under the ocean floor. It is known as the Mohorovicic Discontinuity, after its discoverer. Scientists have nicknamed it the 'Moho'. A seismic wave going down towards the Moho speeds up gradually. But at the Moho it suddenly makes a jump in speed of about 20 miles a minute.

The whole thickness of rock down to the Moho is called the earth's crust. Scientists have a fair idea of its structure. On the continents, the outermost material is a skin mostly of sedimentary rocks, worn through here and there. Under this skin lie rocks of the granite family. Beneath the granite lie rocks that behave like basalt. But under the oceans, the crust has a different structure. There is no granite–only basalt and rocks resembling it, which extend down to the Moho.

Beneath the Moho, wave speeds increase gradually without another jump for 1,800 miles. This whole thick region is called the earth's *mantle*. Then, at the 1,800-mile level, there is a sudden slow-down. This point marks the boundary of the earth's core, which evidently is made of different material from the mantle.

The diagram on page 52 shows how seismologists locate the boundary between mantle and core. Waves from a shock spread through the earth and are picked up by stations at various distances. P-waves are detected on the opposite side of the earth, showing that they go right through the core.

But in a broad zone beginning about 7,300 miles from the earthquake, the waves fade out. This is called the shadow zone. Waves miss it because they bend inwards when

Earthquake waves reveal the earth's structure

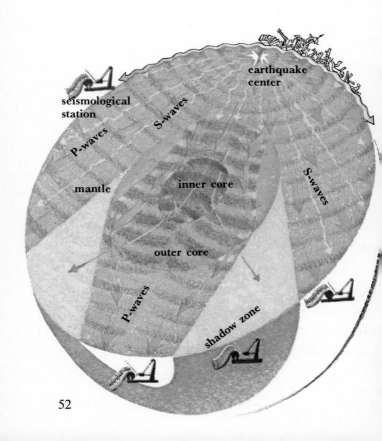

crossing the boundary of the core, and therefore come out farther around towards the opposite side of the earth.

No S-waves are found to pass through the core–only P-waves. This is a clue to the state of the core. P-waves go through a liquid, since it is elastic and jumps back from compression. But S-waves do not go through a liquid, since it does not shake back and forth. Is the earth's core liquid? Scientists say it seems to be.

Another clue about the core is the drop in speed when a wave enters it. This is almost certainly caused by a sudden increase in density, as though the core were made of denser material than the mantle–possibly iron and other heavy metals.

But the core is not the same all the way through. Very faint seismic waves have been picked up in the shadow zone. These probably are echoes from a boundary inside the core. The region beneath the boundary is called the inner core. Scientists think it is made up of metals kept solid by enormous pressure. The seismic messages seem to say: the earth has a heart of iron.

Restless Planet

7. FLOATING CRUST

Two centuries ago, scientists noticed a curious thing about the behaviour of a pendulum clock. When such a clock was taken towards the equator it ran slower. When it was taken away from the equator it ran faster. Why?

GRAVITY AND THE PENDULUM

The earth has a bulge around the equator. Points near the equator are farther from the earth's centre than points elsewhere. The added distance lessens the force of gravity.

A pendulum swings because gravity pulls upon it. The weaker the pull, the slower the swing; the greater the pull, the faster the swing. The pendulum clock ran slower or faster depending on the force of gravity tugging on the pendulum.

As a pendulum goes on swinging, friction gradually brakes the action. The swings

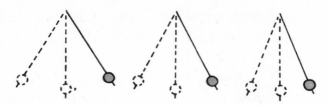

become slower, but they also become narrower, so each swing still takes the same amount of time. This time is called the *period* of the pendulum. It is a good indicator of the force of gravity. Where gravity is greater, the period is shorter. Where gravity is less, the period is longer.

Gravity differences are slight, and cause only slight differences in the period of the pendulum. Therefore, the period must be measured very accurately. It is not enough to time one swing. Instead the pendulum is allowed to make thousands of swings, which are counted automatically. Then the time is divided by the number of swings. This method gives the period to within one ten-millionth of a second.

GRAVITY AND THE SPRING SCALE

The pendulum has drawbacks as a gravity instrument. Several hours are needed to take a measurement. In addition, the instrument is too heavy to be carried by hand. So scientists also use a simpler tool. This is the gravimeter, which is just a sensitive spring scale. The spring is a fine, hairlike coil, from which a small mass hangs. The force of gravity pulling on the mass is shown by the stretching of the spring. With this light, easily-carried instrument, a reading can be taken in a few minutes.

Scientists begin a gravity survey by taking a measurement with the pendulum. This gives them a figure which they use in setting the scale of the gravimeter. Then readings from the scale stand for small variations in gravity.

**A scientist takes
a gravimeter reading**

'WEIGHING' MOUNTAINS

When a scientist has taken a measurement at a certain place, he compares it with the strength of gravity expected at that latitude. This theoretical *value* of gravity is obtained by calculation.

But before making the comparison, he corrects his own figure in certain ways. Suppose he is measuring gravity in the Andes Mountains, at a station a few miles above sea level. This extra distance from the earth's centre lessens the pull of gravity by a certain amount, which the scientist adds to his figure to make it equivalent to a reading taken at sea level.

Secondly, the rock in the mountain between the station and sea level causes an extra amount of pull, which the scientist subtracts from his figure. Now the figure is fully corrected, and can be compared with the theoretical value. Does it agree with this value? It does not. The figure is lower; gravity is weaker than it should be. And it is considerably weaker than gravity in lowland areas of the continent.

In trying to account for this, the scientist

remembers that gravity depends partly on the mass–the weight or quantity of material–under the mountains. Somehow, there is a shortage of mass. This is true of the Andes, and also of the mountains of other continents. Why is gravity weaker in mountains than in lowlands? In pondering this question, scientists began to suspect that a great body of light rock lay under the mountains, as though the earth's crust were thicker there.

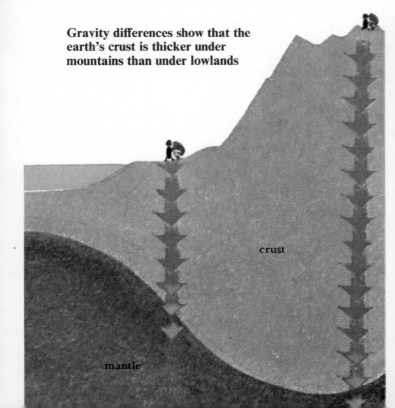

Gravity differences show that the earth's crust is thicker under mountains than under lowlands

crust

mantle

An explosive charge is fired in a Chilean mine

Several years ago scientists from Peru, Chile, and the United States climbed the Andes to measure the thickness of the crust beneath the mountains. Their plan was to take advantage of powerful dynamite blasts set off daily in the copper mines of Chile and Peru. Compression waves from a blast would probably go through the crust, bounce back from the Moho, and return to the surface.

Instruments were set up, the blasts went off, and compression waves were recorded.

The scientists noted how long it took the waves to echo back from the top of the mantle. Their records showed the crust under the mountains to be some 40 miles thick. This is about twice the thickness of the crust in lowland regions.

GRAVITY OF THE OCEANS

When a pendulum was developed for use on board ship, scientists found that the ocean basins have the strongest gravity on earth. Why?

Here, too, gravity is affected by the structure of the crust. Its thickness under the oceans has been measured by seismic shooting. A depth charge explodes, and compression waves from the blast go down through the water, through sediments on the bottom,

A diver measures gravity on the ocean floor

Seismic shooting probes rock under the sea

and through the crust. Echoing from the
Moho, the waves are recorded on board ship.
Their travel time, which is short, shows that
the mantle is not far down. In some areas
it is only three miles beneath the ocean floor.
This helps to explain the strong gravity of
the ocean basins. There the heavy, dense
rock of the mantle lies near the earth's surface, increasing the pull of gravity. In addition, the rock of the ocean floor itself is
heavier and more dense than average rocks
of the continents.

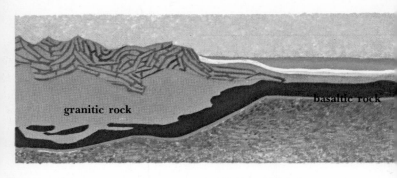

Under the continents, the earth's crust is thick and granitic; under the ocean, it is thin and basaltic

Compression waves from depth charge hit the earth's mantle and bounce back

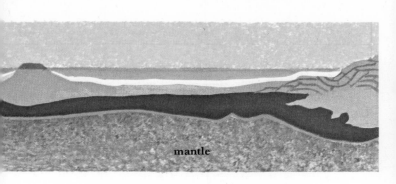

mantle

THE CRUST IN BALANCE

Regions of heavy rock tend to be lowlands. Regions of light rock are highlands. When scientists discovered this, they realized that blocks of the crust behave as though they were floating on the mantle. This does not mean that the mantle is liquid. But very likely it is *plastic*. In this state a material does not break when some force works upon it over a long period of time. Instead, it yields by a slow, oozy sort of flowing. Tar is an example of such material. A block of tar appears solid. It will break when struck with a hammer. But if the hammer is laid on top of the tar and rests there awhile, it gradually sinks in.

Mountain blocks, being lighter than the mantle, rest on it as icebergs float on the sea.

Icebergs extend down into the water, which buoys them up; mountains extend down into the mantle, which buoys them up. As the mountains erode away and become lighter, the pressure of the mantle keeps buoying them up.

The same thing happens to the continents. They are always wearing down as their rocks crumble and rivers carry the fragments to the sea. This has been going on for ages, yet the continents are still high and the ocean basins low. Gravity and the buoyant force of the mantle work together to hold them so. Thus, our planet keeps the great surface features–land and sea–which it has had for thousands of millions of years.

**The earth's crust is buoyed up by the mantle.
Heavy rock areas are low; light rock areas are high**

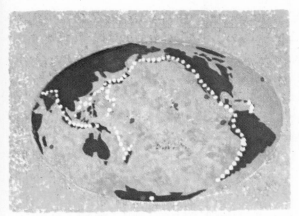

A volcano and earthquake zone encircles the Pacific

8. RING OF FIRE

ALONG the Pacific Coast of the Americas, chains of lofty mountains link end to end for thousands of miles. This giant mountain wall is all the more impressive because it marks a zone of volcanic and seismic activity. Think of the Andes, with their earthquakes and lava floods!

The restless zone parallels the Andes from southern Chile to the Isthmus of Panama–a bridge of volcanoes connecting the Americas. From there it follows the coastal mountains through Mexico, the United States, Canada, and Alaska. Crossing to Asia, the zone runs down the Pacific shore, passes through Japan and Indonesia, then loops under the southern seas. Together, the Asian and American sections of the zone form a vast ring.

Around this 'Ring of Fire' the land and the sea floor are broken in a long series of cracks. Blocks of the crust often shift along the cracks. Some slip horizontally, others rise or sink, and each jolting movement sets off an earthquake. Through breaks opened by these disturbances, hot magma forces its way to the surface. New volcanoes are born; old volcanoes rise higher.

The volcano Izalco, in El Salvador, erupts

The volcano Fujiyama, in Japan, is quiet

Where mountains tower up from the sea, the ocean floor beside them is warped downwards into long trenches. Some of these trenches are deeper than the mountains are high. And some are still sinking as the mountains continue to rise.

What inner commotions trigger the earthquakes and eruptions, raise the mountains, and depress the trenches? These activities around the Ring of Fire seem to be connected with certain upheavals going on under the deep ocean basins.

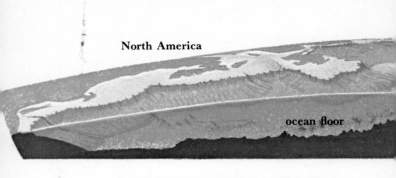

North America

ocean floor

9. CONTINENTS ADRIFT

A CENTURY ago, the shape of the ocean bottom was a mystery. Scientists lacked a good way to investigate it. They could only measure depths with a weighted line, and this was done in just a few places, because lowering and raising the line took a lot of time and effort. And yet, by feeling in the dark North Atlantic with their line, the scientists did detect an important feature. This was a mountain range rising from the middle of the ocean floor.

Recently, scientists devised a much better method of exploration, called echo sounding. An instrument on board ship makes a series of 'pings'–sound impulses that speed through the water in the form of compression waves. These waves hit the bottom, echo back, and

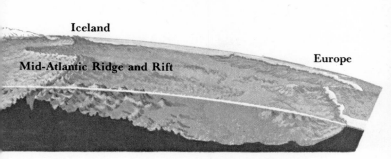

Iceland

Europe

Mid-Atlantic Ridge and Rift

record their travel time in the form of a line. The line goes up and down, following the shape of the bottom.

RIFT IN THE OCEAN FLOOR

Scientists crossed and re-crossed the Atlantic taking profiles with the echo sounder. Working from these profiles, they were able to map the whole bottom. When their map was finished, it revealed a tremendous hidden feature of the earth–a great long ridge of mountains running the entire length of the Atlantic. The ridge divides the ocean basin into a western half, bordered by the Americas, and an eastern half, bordered by Europe and Africa. The profiles show that the ridge is split down most of its length by an enormous rift, deeper and wider than the Grand Canyon of the Colorado River.

69

The ridge rises about two miles from the ocean floor, with summits reaching to within a few thousand feet of the surface. Several peaks emerge above the surface as islands. Among these are the Azores, which are the tops of old volcanoes. Another high portion of the ridge forms Iceland, a lava plateau that is still growing as volcanic eruptions build it up.

The ridge follows a very active seismic zone. Of all the earthquakes traced to the Atlantic basin, nearly all occur in this zone. The shocks come from the rather shallow depth of 18 miles. Evidently, the earth's crust under the ridge is disturbed by forces that continually break it, causing earthquakes and lava eruptions.

Similar ridges have recently been found crossing the floors of the other oceans. These ridges, too, mark zones of earthquake activity. In fact, they were discovered by taking profiles across seismic zones. The ridges of the several oceans link into one connected system 40,000 miles long, forming the earth's third great feature, after the oceans and the continents.

The rift in the Atlantic ridge emerges in plain view in Iceland, where it forms a steep, canyon-like gap across the island. All of Iceland's recent volcanic eruptions have occurred along this gap, as have nearly all of its earthquakes. Deep cracks along the gap are slowly opening wider, and the gap as a whole is spreading by about two inches a year.

Cracks are opening in the rift across Iceland

It seems that for a long time the earth's crust has been splitting and spreading along the whole length of the rift. Volcanic islands near it are made of very young rocks. Farther away on both sides, the islands are older. The distant islands as well as the near ones probably were born from the ridge and rift, and were carried away from it by the spreading of the earth's crust. By comparing the ages of the islands and their distances from the rift, scientists find that the average rate of movement has been an inch and a half a year.

What causes the spreading of the crust

along the ridge-rift? One clue is found in the nature of its material. Earthquake waves go through the ridge at high speeds, indicating heavy, dense rocks. Among samples dredged from the ridge are rocks even heavier and denser than basalt. Such rocks probably make up the earth's mantle. This evidence suggests that dense material from the mantle has been rising under the ridge-rift. This upward movement apparently breaks the crust and widens the rift.

In determining the age of rock, a sample is crushed; then, products formed by radioactive decay are separated and measured

Temperatures deep in the ridge-rift are taken by lowering instruments from ships

Another clue comes from temperatures in the ridge-rift, which show the rate at which heat from the interior flows up through it. The rate of heat flow is several times greater than in the flat ocean floor and the continents. From this we may conclude that hot material from the mantle is rising under the ridge-rift.

A very different situation exists along the trenches that parallel the shores of the Pacific. There the rate of heat flow is low, and so are gravity values. These facts suggest that cold, light material of the crust is being pulled down under the trenches. Earthquakes are frequent there, but not at shallow levels. All occur several hundred miles down. Even at such depths, the rock is solid enough to break rather than flow. Why? Presumably because it is cold, solid stuff sinking from upper levels.

According to this picture of events, the earth's mantle is stirred by vast slow currents that rise under the rifts and sink under the trenches. The currents are set in motion by temperature differences in the mantle. In a colder zone, material sinks because it is denser and heavier. In a hotter zone, material rises because it is lighter. Where a rising current approaches the top of the mantle, it spreads out on both sides and pulls the crust apart.

MIGRATING CONTINENTS

The picture of a splitting, spreading crust agrees with an idea proposed over fifty years ago by the German scientist, Alfred Wegener. He argued that the continents originally were joined in a single mass and later drifted apart.

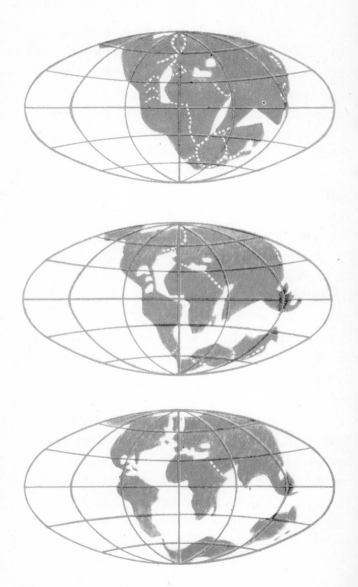

According to the theory of continental drift, all the earth's land was once joined in a single mass. Later the land mass split into sections that drifted apart, forming the continents

The eastern edges of the Americas match the western edges of Europe and Africa fairly well. Australia and other land bodies of the southern hemisphere also have nearly matching shapes, and although separated now by the sea, they have similar fossils. The shapes of the world's continents suggest that they were formerly joined. By rearranging the world map, we can fit the Americas in with Europe and Africa like pieces of a rough jigsaw puzzle.

Wegener's idea is supported by evidence from ancient basalt rocks. When these rocks were forming from a rock melt, grains of iron minerals in them became magnetized and lined up like compass needles pointing towards the earth's north magnetic pole. The grains froze in position, and have remained so to this day. But now the grains in some of the rocks do not point to the magnetic pole, and on different continents the grains point in different directions. Apparently, either

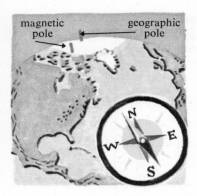

**A compass needle points
to the north magnetic pole**

the magnetic pole or the land masses–or both–
have shifted.

It is known that the magnetic pole does
shift; it is shifting today. Even so, magnetic
grains in rocks of the same age on different
continents point in different directions. Originally, all must have pointed in one direction–
towards the magnetic pole of that period of
the earth's history. Thus, it appears that land
masses have indeed shifted. A few scientists
are still not convinced, but the evidence is
strong.

Some scientists think the continents were

moved by currents in the mantle. Others believe that the earth may be expanding as the interior heats up from radioactivity. If this is so, the continents are gradually moving apart as the earth expands–like spots on a balloon when the balloon is blown up.

In any case, the key to the puzzle lies under the ocean floor. As scientists go on exploring, they will uncover further secrets of the forces that change our world.

Before long, submersibles will carry scientists on trips along the deep ocean floor

INDEX